Life Around the World

What Are Homes Like Around the World?

By Kathleen Connors

New York

Published in 2022 by Cavendish Square Publishing, LLC
243 5th Avenue, Suite 136, New York, NY 10016

Copyright © 2022 by Cavendish Square Publishing, LLC

First Edition

No part of this publication may be reproduced, stored in a retrieval system, or transmitted in any form or by any means—electronic, mechanical, photocopying, recording, or otherwise—without the prior permission of the copyright owner. Request for permission should be addressed to Permissions, Cavendish Square Publishing, 243 5th Avenue, Suite 136, New York, NY 10016.
Tel (877) 980-4450; fax (877) 980-4454.

Website: cavendishsq.com

This publication represents the opinions and views of the author based on his or her personal experience, knowledge, and research. The information in this book serves as a general guide only. The author and publisher have used their best efforts in preparing this book and disclaim liability rising directly or indirectly from the use and application of this book.

All websites were available and accurate when this book was sent to press.

Library of Congress Cataloging-in-Publication Data
Names: Connors, Kathleen, author.
Title: What are homes like around the world? / Kathleen Connors.
Description: New York : Cavendish Square Publishing, [2022] | Series: Life around the world | Includes index.
Identifiers: LCCN 2020031844 | ISBN 9781502659361 (library binding) | ISBN 9781502659347 (paperback) | ISBN 9781502659354 (set) | ISBN 9781502659378 (ebook)
Subjects: LCSH: Dwellings–Juvenile literature.
Classification: LCC GT172 .C66 2022 | DDC 392.3/6–dc23
LC record available at https://lccn.loc.gov/2020031844

Editor: Kristen Nelson
Designer: Tanya Dellaccio

The photographs in this book are used by permission and through the courtesy of: Cover Faer Out/Shutterstock.com; p. 5 (top left) Douglas Keister/Corbis Documentary/Getty Images; pp. 5 (top right), 7 Alexander Spatari/Moment/Getty Images; p. 5 (bottom left) icholakov/iStock/Getty Images Plus/Getty Images; p. 5 (bottom right) Westend61/Getty Images; p. 9 Blissography/iStock/Getty Images Plus/Getty Images; p. 11 Delmas Lehman/iStock/Getty Images Plus/Getty Images; p. 13 Kanda Dp/EyeEm/Getty Images; p. 15 pjjones/iStock/Getty Images Plus/Getty Images; p. 17 Barry Kusuma/Photolibrary/Getty Images Plus/Getty Images; p. 19 RobertBreitpaul/iStock/Getty Images Plus/Getty Images; p. 21 Ryan McVay/DigitalVision/Getty Images; p. 23 Ariel Skelley/DigitalVision/Getty Images.

Some of the images in this book illustrate individuals who are models. The depictions do not imply actual situations or events.

CPSIA compliance information: Batch #CS22CSQ: For further information contact Cavendish Square Publishing LLC, New York, New York, at 1-877-980-4450.

Printed in the United States of America

CONTENTS

Many Kinds of Homes	4
What's It Made Of?	8
Off the Ground	14
Words to Know	24
Index	24

Many Kinds of Homes

People in the United States live in many kinds of homes. Some live in houses for one family. Others live in apartment buildings. People may live in homes on wheels or even on boats! What are homes like in other countries?

Homes in Great Britain are much like those in the United States. Many people in cities live in apartments, which they call flats. Towns also have homes that are all **attached**. These are called terraced houses.

What's It Made Of?

Different kinds of homes are made of different things. **Traditional** homes in Mexico and the southwestern United States are made of adobe. Adobe is a brick made of clay, straw, and water that has been dried in the sun.

Uganda is a country in eastern Africa. Homes in the countryside there are small and shaped like a circle. The walls are made of mud. The roof may be made of straw or grass, or made of a sheet of iron.

Traditional homes in Thailand are made of wood and the bamboo plant. They have **pitched** roofs that hang over the sides of outside walls. Thailand gets a lot of rain. These roofs help the rain roll off easily!

Off the Ground

Thai houses are often up on **stilts** too. Stilts are part of other countries' homes as well. One kind from Australia is called the Queenslander. It's built raised to keep the house safe from flooding.

In the island nation of Indonesia, many people's homes are right on the water. These homes are on stilts too! This keeps the houses dry and cool. It also keeps those living there away from bugs like mosquitoes.

Some homes are raised sky high! Apartment buildings in the United Arab Emirates can have as many as 100 floors. Princess Tower in Dubai, United Arab Emirates, is one of the tallest buildings in the world people live in!

In Japan, more and more people are moving into tall apartment buildings too. Others live in homes not that different from those found in the United States. There's one main difference, though. Shoes are never worn inside a Japanese home!

Homes around the world may be different from place to place. Who lives inside a home is what matters most, though. The people inside a house, apartment, or hut are what make a place home!

WORDS TO KNOW

attached: Connected or joined.

pitched: Having a slope.

stilts: A set of posts used to hold a building up above water or the ground.

traditional: Following what's been done for a long time.

INDEX

A
adobe, 8
apartments, 4, 6, 18, 20
Australia, 14

G
Great Britain, 6

I
Indonesia, 16

J
Japan, 20

M
Mexico, 8

T
terraced houses, 6
Thailand, 12, 14

U
Uganda, 10
United Arab Emirates, 18
United States, 4, 6, 20